K12 Publishing

Dolch Sight Words Practice – Book 1

Fun and interesting activities to help your student in pre-kindergarten through first grade learn 105 high-frequency pre-primer and primer Dolch sight words.

ISBN-10: 0-9965219-1-7

ISBN-13: 978-0-9965219-1-8

Table of Contents

About the Workbook

This sight word workbook contains activities for 105 Dolch sight words. These 105 words include 80 words from the pre-primer and primer levels and 25 nouns. They are the most basic words a child needs to know to learn to read.

What Are Sight Words?

Sight words are words commonly used in texts, such as the words *and, is,* and *the.* These common words are estimated to make up over half of the words in a student's textbook, in a newspaper, and in reading books.

In 1948 Edward William Dolch published a list of English words he had compiled from analyzing children's books. He identified 220 non-nouns and 95 nouns that commonly appeared in the texts. He classified these into five levels: pre-primer, primer, first, second, and third. The Dolch sight word list has been used successfully to teach reading for over 60 years.

The words are called sight words because if readers can instantly recognize them, reading fluency and comprehension increases. Many of the words on the list are not able to be decoded by a reader using common reading strategies such as phonetics or "sounding out." For example, *down* and *own* are both on the Dolch list. They appear to be rhyming words when they are not. Another example is *two,* which sounds nonsensical if it is pronounced phonetically.

Why Are Sight Words Important?

Sight words increase reading fluency, or reading speed, accuracy and comprehension. If a child starts a story already knowing over half the words "by sight," then he or she will be able to concentrate more fully on the unknown words. This is especially important for words that are used often but may be difficult to decode as mentioned previously.

Fluent readers are also able to better understand what they read. They are able to group words together quickly and comprehend the meaning of phrases and sentences. Instead of slowly reading one word at a time, they can read whole sentences and understand them.

The Activities

Sight word practice is not the same as spelling drills. Spelling drills concentrate on less commonly used words and spelling rules. The key to sight words is visualization. A student should ultimately see the word and know it without sounding it out or even pausing. These words should become second-nature to the reader. With this in mind, the activities in the book are geared to visual recognition.

The individual word activities focus on one sight word each. The student is asked to write the word alone and in a sentence. The goal of these exercises is to impress upon the student the individual letters that make up the whole word. The student is then asked to identify the word as a stand-alone word and in a sentence. These activities strengthen the visual recognition of the word.

Also included in this workbook are multiple word activities. All 105 words are included in one of the multiple word activities. These practice pages are designed to reinforce visual recognition of the sight words when they appear among others. Some activities, such as Color the Sight Word or Animal Fun, spotlight one word. Other activities, such as Sight Word Color by Number or Spot the Sight Words use two or more sight words together.

Tips for Teaching Sight Words

1. Interaction

Depending on the student and the reading skill level, these activities can be done by the student alone or with support and guidance from an adult. If working with the student, an adult may want to add a verbal component to each exercise, such as asking the student to repeat the word aloud after writing it. Asking the student to spell the word aloud is also a useful strategy.

Each activity is interactive, meaning the student has some physical action (writing, coloring, etc.) to perform on each page. These physical actions are intended to keep the student engaged throughout the activity. When working together on a page, the adult could perform some of the physical actions as directed by the student. For example, in the Color the Sight Word activities, the student could color the focus word, and the adult could color another word chosen and identified by the student.

2. Pacing

Some words, such as the single-letter words *a* and *I*, may come easily to the student. Others, such as *where* and *yellow*, may be a greater challenge. Rather than using the words in alphabetical order, an alternative strategy might be to start with the simplest words or words the student already knows. As the student is successful with those activities, move up to the more challenging ones.

Another useful strategy may be to vary the activities frequently. This strategy would call for the student to complete about five to seven individual word activities, followed by one of the multiple word activities.

3. Evaluation and Feedback

Swift evaluation of a student's completed activity is essential. A discussion of correct and incorrect answers when the activity is still fresh in the student's mind is an important component for success. It also allows the adult to evaluate possible challenges the student is having in recognizing the words.

Positive reinforcement is also a vital component for early readers. Missed answers and errors should be clarified, but correct answers should also be noted and reinforced. Displaying the Color the Sight Word activity is also an excellent way to reinforce and celebrate a well-completed activity.

Finally, please remember that the activity sheets can be duplicated if there is a particular word or words the student finds challenging. It might be helpful to complete other words before repeating the same exercise.

Individual Word Activities

Sight Word Practice: A

Write the Word: **a**

_____   _____

_____   _____

_____   _____

Fill in the Sentence

Fill in the blanks to make the word **a**.

I have _____ dog.

He gave me _____ toy.

_____ girl sat under the tree.

Circle the Word

Circle the flowers that have the word **a**.

Circle the Word in the Sentence

Circle the word **a** in the sentences.

They ran a race.   I want a ball.

Name: _____

Sight Word Practice: All

Write the word: all

_____   _____

- - - - - - - -   - - - - - - - -

_____   _____

Fill in the Sentence

Fill in the blanks to make the word **all**.

She saw _____ _____ _____
of the show.

_____ _____ _____ cats have
four legs.

We bought _____ _____ _____
the toys.

Circle the Word

Circle the flowers that have the word **all**.

Circle the Word in the Sentence

Circle the word **all** in the sentences.

He ran all the way home.

Do you want all of the grapes?

Name: _____

Sight Word Practice: Am

Write the Word: am

am

_____ _____

- - - - - - - - - - - - - - - - - - - -

_____ _____

Fill in the Sentence

Fill in the blanks to make the word **am**.

I _____ _____ hungry.

Where _____ _____ I?

I _____ _____ ready to go.

Circle the Word

Circle the flowers that have the word **am**.

Circle the Word in the Sentence

Circle the word **am** in the sentences.

I am late for dinner.

Am I your best friend?

Name: _____

Sight Word Practice: and

Write the Word: **and**

and

_____   _____

- -

_____   _____

Fill in the Sentence

Fill in the blanks to make the word **and**.

The hat was blue ____ ____ ____ red.

John ____ ____ ____ Mary went to the store.

They are nice ____ ____ ____ friendly.

Circle the Word

Circle the flowers that have the word **and**.

Circle the Word in the Sentence

Circle the word **and** in the sentences.

We ran and played after school.

The cat was soft and warm.

Name: _____

Sight Word Practice: Are

Write the word: **are**

_____   _____

- - - - - - - - - - - - - - - - - -

_____   _____

Fill in the Sentence

Fill in the blanks to make the word **are**.

They ____ ____ ____ good players.

We ____ ____ ____ eating outside.

The cows ____ ____ ____ happy in the barn.

Circle the Word

Circle the flowers that have the word **are**.

Circle the Word in the Sentence

Circle the word **are** in the sentences.

The boys are late today.   Are you going home?

Name: _____

Sight Word Practice: At

Write the word: **at**

_____   _____

- - - - - - - - - - -   - - - - - - - - - - -

_____   _____

Fill in the Sentence

Fill in the blanks to make the word **at**.

I will meet you _____ _____ noon.

We have fun _____ _____ the beach.

The cat was _____ _____ the door.

Circle the Word

Circle the flowers that have the word **at**.

Circle the Word in the Sentence

Circle the word **at** in the sentences.

They were at the store. He can't sing at all.

Name: _____

Sight Word Practice: Away

Write the Word: **away**

_____

_____

_____

_____

Fill in the Sentence

Fill in the blanks to make the word **away**.

He walked ____ ____ ____ ____.

The horse ran

____ ____ ____ ____ from the fire.

She will go ____ ____ ____ ____
for the summer.

Circle the Word

Circle the flowers that have the word **away**.

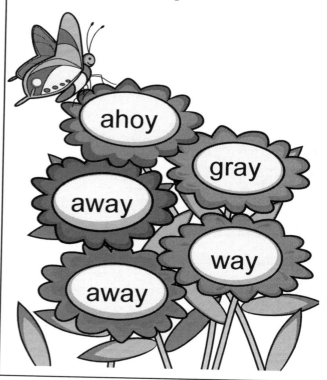

Circle the Word in the Sentence

Circle the word **away** in the sentences.

The mice played when the cat was away.

Please put your toys away.

Sight Word Practice: Baby

Write the Word: **baby**

_____   _____

- - - - - - - - - - - - - - -   - - - - - - - - - - - - - -

- - - - - - - - - - - - - - -   - - - - - - - - - - - - - -

Fill in the Sentence

Fill in the blanks to make the word **baby**.

The ____ ____ ____ ____

cried all day.

I have a ____ ____ ____ ____

sister.

The ____ ____ ____ ____ had a

white hat.

Circle the Word

Circle the flowers that have the word **baby**.

Circle the Word in the Sentence

Circle the word **baby** in the sentences.

The baby wore blue shoes.   Where is the baby?

Name: _____

Sight Word Practice: Ball

Write the Word: **ball**

ball

_____   _____

_____   _____

Fill in the Sentence

Fill in the blanks to make the word **ball**.

He threw the ____ ____ ____ ____ .

The ____ ____ ____ ____ is blue.

My ____ ____ ____ ____ is lost.

Circle the Word

Circle the flowers that have the word **ball**.

Circle the Word in the Sentence

Circle the word **ball** in the sentences.

She gave the ball to me.   Where is the ball?

Name: _____

Sight Word Practice: Be

Write the word: **be**

_____   _____

- - - - - - - - -   - - - - - - - - -

_____   _____

Fill in the Sentence

Fill in the blanks to make the word **be**.

Do you want to _____ _____ my friend?

I can _____ _____ the best.

Where will you _____ _____ ?

Circle the Word

Circle the flowers that have the word **be**.

Circle the Word in the Sentence

Circle the word **be** in the sentences.

We will be late.   She must be sad.

Name: _____

Sight Word Practice: Bed

Write the Word: **bed**

bed _____   _____

Fill in the Sentence

Fill in the blanks to make the word **bed**.

She will sleep in

that ____ ____ ____ .

My ____ ____ ____ is very big.

His cat sleeps in a soft

____ ____ ____.

Circle the Word

Circle the flowers that have the word **bed**.

Circle the Word in the Sentence

Circle the word **bed** in the sentences.

We looked under the bed for the toy.

The bed had a yellow pillow on it.

Name: _____

Sight Word Practice: Big

Write the Word: **big**

big

------ ------ ------ ------

Fill in the Sentence

Fill in the blanks to make the word **big**.

She saw a ____ ____ ____ cow.

The ____ ____ ____ tree fell on the house.

We ate a ____ ____ ____ dinner.

Circle the Word

Circle the flowers that have the word **big**.

Circle the Word in the Sentence

Circle the word **big** in the sentences.

The rock was very big.   My big sister is nice.

Name: _____

Sight Word Practice: Black

Write the Word: **black**

_____
_____
_____
_____

black

Fill in the Sentence

Fill in the blanks to make the word **black**.

The ____ ____ ____ ____ ____
dog slept on the floor.

She has

____ ____ ____ ____ ____ hair.

We have a new

____ ____ ____ ____ ____ car.

Circle the Word

Circle the flowers that have the word **black**.

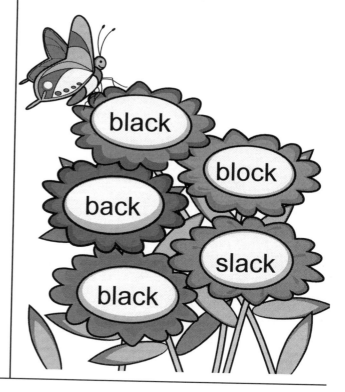

Circle the Word in the Sentence

Circle the word **black** in the sentences.

It was a black night with no moon.

A zebra is black and white.

Name: _____

Sight Word Practice: Blue

Write the Word: **blue**

blue _____ _____

_____ _____

Fill in the Sentence

Fill in the blanks to make the word **blue**.

She has ____ ____ ____ ____ eyes.

The ____ ____ ____ ____ book is mine.

The sky is ____ ____ ____ ____.

Circle the Word

Circle the flowers that have the word **blue**.

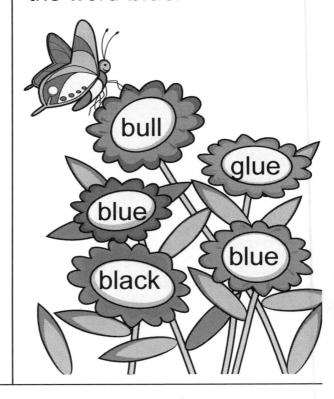

Circle the Word in the Sentence

Circle the word **blue** in the sentences.

Blue is my favorite color.   They have a blue car.

Name: _____

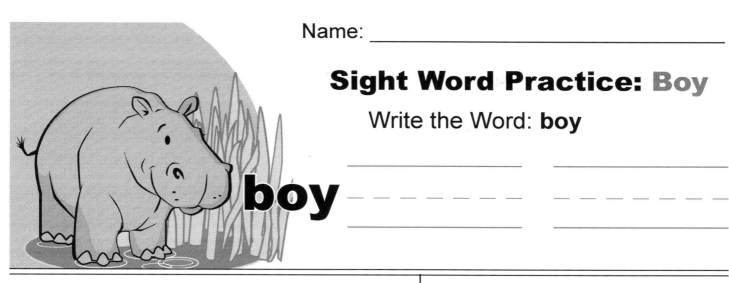

Sight Word Practice: Boy

Write the Word: **boy**

boy

_____ _____

_____ _____

Fill in the Sentence

Fill in the blanks to make the word **boy**.

The ____ ____ ____ is named Jack.

We saw a ____ ____ ____ at the store.

That ____ ____ ____ runs fast.

Circle the Word

Circle the flowers that have the word **boy**.

Circle the Word in the Sentence

Circle the word **boy** in the sentences.

The boy played in the snow.   Do you see the boy over there?

Sight Word Practice: Brown

Write the Word: **brown**

_____
_____
_____
_____

Fill in the Sentence

Fill in the blanks to make the word **brown**.

His eyes are

____ ____ ____ ____ ____.

The ____ ____ ____ ____ ____
cow ate some grass.

I broke the

___ ____ ____ ____ ____ crayon.

Circle the Word

Circle the flowers that have the word **brown**.

Circle the Word in the Sentence

Circle the word **brown** in the sentences.

They painted their house brown.

She sat on the brown chair.

Name: _____

Sight Word Practice: But

Write the word: **but**

but _____ _____

_____ _____

_____ _____

Fill in the Sentence

Fill in the blanks to make the word **but**.

She is fast, _____ _____ _____
I am faster.

We were late, _____ _____ _____
John was early.

No one _____ _____ _____
Bill can pet the dog.

Circle the Word

Circle the flowers that have the word **but**.

Circle the Word in the Sentence

Circle the word **but** in the sentences.

I want to go, but my mother said no.

He wanted a blue bike, but he got a green one.

Name: _____

Sight Word Practice: Cake

Write the Word: cake

cake

_____   _____

_____   _____

_____   _____

Fill in the Sentence

Fill in the blanks to make the word **cake**.

We ate ____ ____ ____ ____

at the party.

The ____ ____ ____ ____ was

pink and green.

I like to eat ____ ____ ____ ____.

Circle the Word

Circle the flowers that have the word **cake**.

Circle the Word in the Sentence

Circle the word **cake** in the sentences.

The cake had red flowers on it.

She made a cake today.

Name: _____

Sight Word Practice: Came

Write the Word: came

_____

_____

_____

Fill in the Sentence

Fill in the blanks to make the word **came**.

She ____ ____ ____ ____ to school early.

The rope ____ ____ ____ ____ loose on the boat.

I ____ ____ ____ ____ close to winning the race.

Circle the Word

Circle the flowers that have the word **came**.

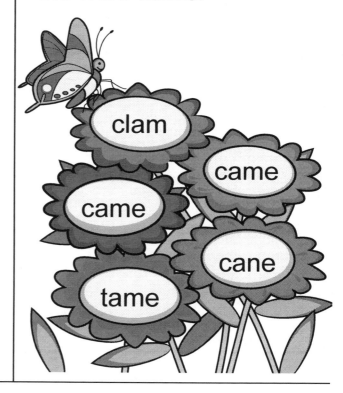

clam

came

came

cane

tame

Circle the Word in the Sentence

Circle the word **came** in the sentences.

He came in the store to buy toys.

I came to ask your help.

Name: _____

Sight Word Practice: Can

Write the Word: **can**

can

_____   _____

- - - - - - - - - - - -   - - - - - - - - - - - -

_____   _____

Fill in the Sentence

Fill in the blanks to make the word **can**.

I ____ ____ ____ run fast.

She has a ____ ____ ____ of soda.

They ____ ____ ____ sing the song.

Circle the Word

Circle the flowers that have the word **can**.

Circle the Word in the Sentence

Circle the word **can** in the sentences.

The dog can live with us.

Can you please help me?

28

Sight Word Practice: Car

Write the Word: car

car

_____ _____

_ _ _ _ _ _ _ _ _ _ _ _ _ _

_____

Fill in the Sentence

Fill in the blanks to make the word **car**.

She saw a ____ ____ ____

drive away.

The ____ ____ ____ is red.

Where is the ____ ____ ____ ?

Circle the Word

Circle the flowers that have the word **car**.

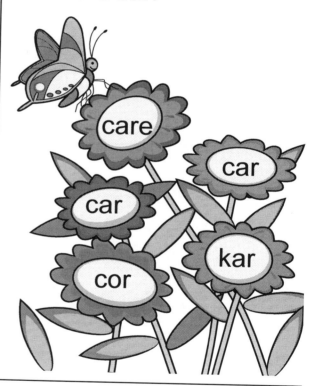

Circle the Word in the Sentence

Circle the word **car** in the sentences.

My mother has a new car.　　A blue car went up the street.

Name: _____

Sight Word Practice: Cat

Write the Word: **cat**

cat

Fill in the Sentence

Fill in the blanks to make the word **cat**.

My ____ ____ ____ likes to sleep.

The ____ ____ ____ sat on the bed.

The dog ran after the

____ ____ ____ .

Circle the Word

Circle the flowers that have the word **cat**.

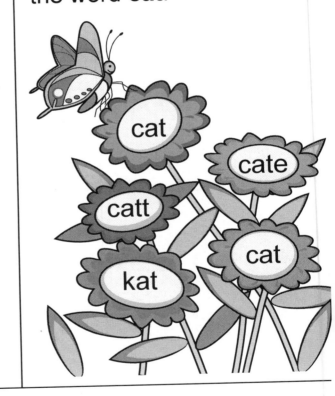

Circle the Word in the Sentence

Circle the word **cat** in the sentences.

Her cat is black and white.   He gave the cat a bath.

come

Name: _____

Sight Word Practice: Come

Write the Word: come

_____

_____

_____

Fill in the Sentence

Fill in the blanks to make the word **come**.

She will ____ ____ ____ ____ to the party.

My cat has ____ ____ ____ ____ home.

Please ____ ____ ____ ____ here.

Circle the Word

Circle the flowers that have the word **come**.

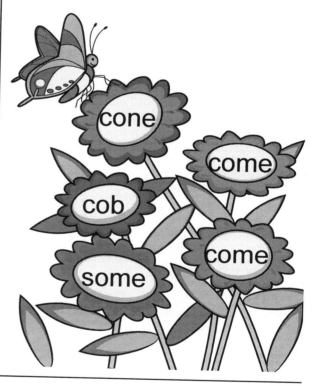

Circle the Word in the Sentence

Circle the word **come** in the sentences.

They wanted us to come outside.

May I come with you?

Name: _____

Sight Word Practice: Cow

Write the Word: **cow**

COW _____

_ _ _ _ _ _ _ _ _ _ _ _ _ _

_____

Fill in the Sentence

Fill in the blanks to make the word **cow**.

The ____ ____ ____ ate the grass.

He saw a ____ ____ ____ on the farm.

The ____ ____ ____ was in the barn

Circle the Word

Circle the flowers that have the word **cow**.

Circle the Word in the Sentence

Circle the word **cow** in the sentences.

We drank the milk from the cow.

That cow is brown and white.

Sight Word Practice: Day

Write the Word: **day**

day

_____ _____

_____ _____

_____ _____

Fill in the Sentence

Fill in the blanks to make the word **day**.

It was a cold ____ ____ ____.

The ____ ____ ____ began early.

What ____ ____ ____ is the party?

Circle the Word

Circle the flowers that have the word **day**.

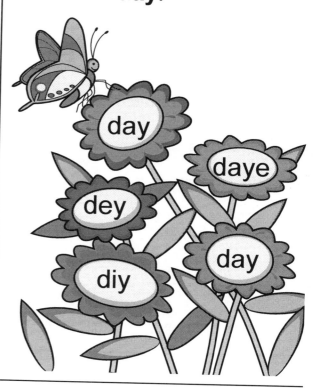

Circle the Word in the Sentence

Circle the word **day** in the sentences.

She worked in the barn all day.

We like to swim on a hot day.

Sight Word Practice: Did

Write the Word: **did**

did

_____ _____

- - - - - - - - - - - - - - - - - - - -

_____ _____

Fill in the Sentence

Fill in the blanks to make the word **did**.

She ____ ____ ____ not want to go.

He ____ ____ ____ the dishes after dinner.

____ ____ ____ you like the story?

Circle the Word

Circle the flowers that have the word **did**.

Circle the Word in the Sentence

Circle the word **did** in the sentences.

Did you see the moon last night?

They did their best on the test.

Name: _____

Sight Word Practice: Do

Write the word: **do**

_____   _____

- -

_____   _____

Fill in the Sentence

Fill in the blanks to make the word **do**.

I _____ _____ not have time today.

Are you ready to _____ _____
the dishes?

He can _____ _____ it better than me.

Circle the Word

Circle the flowers that have the word **do**.

Circle the Word in the Sentence

Circle the word **do** in the sentences.

Do you like me?   You will do it well.

35

Name: _____

Sight Word Practice: Dog

Write the Word: **dog**

dog

_____   _____

- - - - - - - - - -   - - - - - - - - - -

_____   _____

Fill in the Sentence

Fill in the blanks to make the word **dog**.

We have a big ____ ____ ____.

His ____ ____ ____ barks at cats.

She can pet my ____ ____ ____.

Circle the Word

Circle the flowers that have the word **dog**.

Circle the Word in the Sentence

Circle the word **dog** in the sentences.

The dog did a trick.

We played with our dog in the park.

down

Name: _____

Sight Word Practice: Down

Write the Word: **down**

_____ _____

- - - - - - - - - - - - - - - - - - - - - - - - - - - - - -

_____ _____

Fill in the Sentence

Fill in the blanks to make the word **down**.

You may sit

____ ____ ____ ____.

We walked ____ ____ ____ ____
the road.

She looked ____ ____ ____ ____
at her feet.

Circle the Word

Circle the flowers that have the word **down**.

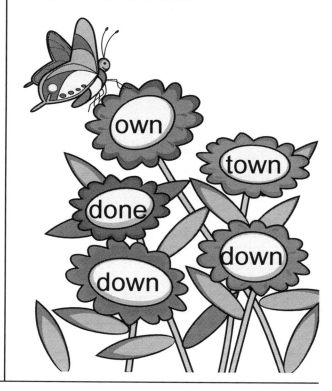

Circle the Word in the Sentence

Circle the word **down** in the sentences.

Please put the book down.

He fell down the steps.

Name: _____

Sight Word Practice: Duck

Write the Word: duck

duck

_____ _____

_____ _____

Fill in the Sentence

Fill in the blanks to make the word **duck**.

The ____ ____ ____ ____ is white.

He saw a ____ ____ ____ ____ in the lake.

I have a ____ ____ ____ ____ as a pet.

Circle the Word

Circle the flowers that have the word **duck**.

Circle the Word in the Sentence

Circle the word **duck** in the sentences.

The duck flew away. A brown duck was in the garden.

Name: _____

Sight Word Practice: Eat

Write the Word: **eat**

eat

_____   _____

- - - - - - - - - -   - - - - - - - - - -

_____   _____

Fill in the Sentence

Fill in the blanks to make the word **eat**.

We ____ ____ ____ fruit.

They can ____ ____ ____ soon.

I will ____ ____ ____ the bread.

Circle the Word

Circle the flowers that have the word **eat**.

Circle the Word in the Sentence

Circle the word **eat** in the sentences.

He wants to eat the cake. Where do you eat lunch?

Name: _____

Sight Word Practice: Find

Write the Word: **find**

find

_ _ _ _ _ _ _ _   _ _ _ _ _ _ _ _

Fill in the Sentence

Fill in the blanks to make the word **find**.

She can not ____ ____ ____ ____ her cat.

He will ____ ____ ____ ____ a new way to school.

I did not ____ ____ ____ ____ my lost book.

Circle the Word

Circle the flowers that have the word **find**.

Circle the Word in the Sentence

Circle the word **find** in the sentences.

She will find the other students nice.

Did you find a penny on the floor?

Sight Word Practice: Fire

Write the Word: **fire**

_____ _____

_ _ _ _ _ _ _ _ _ _ _ _ _ _ _ _ _ _

_____ _____

Fill in the Sentence

Fill in the blanks to make the word **fire**.

She saw the forest

_____ _____ _____ _____.

The _____ _____ _____ _____

is hot.

The _____ _____ _____ _____ truck

went very fast.

Circle the Word

Circle the flowers that have the word **fire**.

Circle the Word in the Sentence

Circle the word **fire** in the sentences.

That house is on fire!   He put sand on the fire.

Name: _____

Sight Word Practice: For

Write the word: **for**

_____ _____

- -

_____ _____

Fill in the Sentence

Fill in the blanks to make the word **for**.

They asked ____ ____ ____ help.

He felt happy ____ ____ ____ her.

The man asked ____ ____ ____ the book.

Circle the Word

Circle the flowers that have the word **for**.

Circle the Word in the Sentence

Circle the word **for** in the sentences.

The house is for sale.   We are looking for our dog.

Name: _____

Sight Word Practice: Four

Write the Word: **four**

four _____   _____

Fill in the Sentence

Fill in the blanks to make the word **four**.

A horse has ____ ____ ____ ____ legs.

The show starts at

____ ____ ____ ____ o'clock.

The ____ ____ ____ ____ ducks swam in the lake.

Circle the Word

Circle the flowers that have the word **four**.

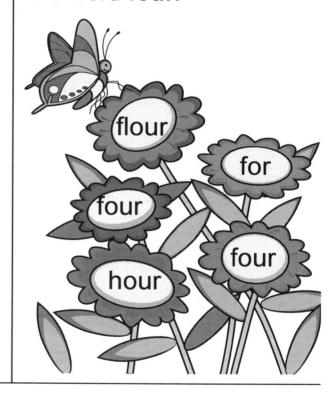

Circle the Word in the Sentence

Circle the word **four** in the sentences.

He saw four cars.   The four girls walked home.

Sight Word Practice: Funny

Write the Word: **funny**

_____

_____

_____

funny

Fill in the Sentence

Fill in the blanks to make the word **funny**.

They saw a

____ ____ ____ ____ ____ clown.

A ____ ____ ____ ____ ____ duck
walked on the road.

I thought the show was

____ ____ ____ ____ ____ .

Circle the Word

Circle the flowers that have the word **funny**.

funny

money

funny

fine

bunny

Circle the Word in the Sentence

Circle the word **funny** in the sentences.

There was a funny noise outside.

She told me a funny joke.

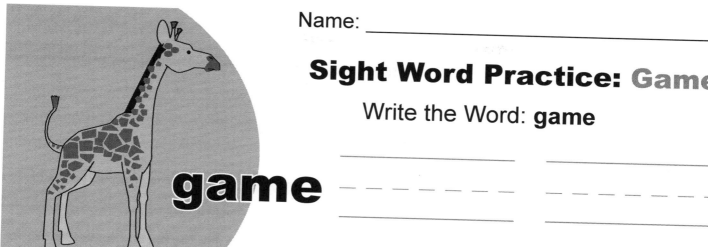

Sight Word Practice: Game

Write the Word: game

game

Fill in the Sentence

Fill in the blanks to make the word **game**.

We played a ___ ___ ___ ___ .

This ___ ___ ___ ___ is fun.

They saw the ___ ___ ___ ___
on TV.

Circle the Word

Circle the flowers that have the word **game**.

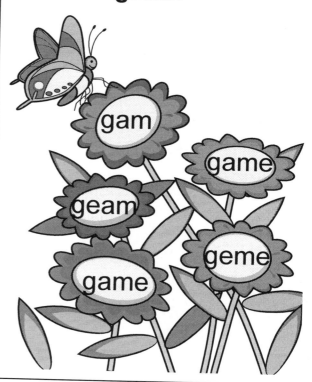

Circle the Word in the Sentence

Circle the word **game** in the sentences.

He won the game.   I have a new game.

Sight Word Practice: Get

Write the Word: **get**

get _____ _____

Fill in the Sentence

Fill in the blanks to make the word **get**.

We want to ____ ____ ____ a cat soon.

He might ____ ____ ____ sick in the cold snow.

I ____ ____ ____ sleepy after lunch.

Circle the Word

Circle the flowers that have the word **get**.

Circle the Word in the Sentence

Circle the word **get** in the sentences.

Get away from the fire!

Did you get a good grade?

Name: _____

Sight Word Practice: Girl

Write the Word: **girl**

girl

- - - - - - - - -   - - - - - - - - -

- - - - - - - - -   - - - - - - - - -

Fill in the Sentence

Fill in the blanks to make the word **girl**.

The ____ ____ ____ ____ wore a red dress.

I don't know that

____ ____ ____ ____.

He told the ____ ____ ____ ____ a story.

Circle the Word

Circle the flowers that have the word **girl**.

Circle the Word in the Sentence

Circle the word **girl** in the sentences.

We played on the swings with a girl.

The girl walked slowly to her house.

47

Name: _____

Sight Word Practice: Go

Write the Word: **go**

go

_____   _____

_ _ _ _ _ _ _ _ _   _ _ _ _ _ _ _ _ _

_____   _____

Fill in the Sentence

Fill in the blanks to make the word **go**.

I like to _____ _____ to school.

She wants to _____ _____ with us.

We can _____ _____ soon.

Circle the Word

Circle the flowers that have the word **go**.

Circle the Word in the Sentence

Circle the word **go** in the sentences.

He must go home.   Did you go to the show?

Sight Word Practice: Good

Write the Word: **good**

good

_____
_ _ _ _ _ _ _ _ _ _ _ _ _
_____
_ _ _ _ _ _ _ _ _ _ _ _ _
_____

Fill in the Sentence

Fill in the blanks to make the word **good**.

He is a ____ ____ ____ ____
friend.

We got some ____ ____ ____ ____
news.

They had a ____ ____ ____ ____
time at the party.

Circle the Word

Circle the flowers that have the word **good**.

goat

good

hood

good

dog

Circle the Word in the Sentence

Circle the word **good** in the sentences.

A good student works hard.

She told a good story.

Name: _____

Sight Word Practice: Hand

Write the Word: **hand**

_____ _____

_____ _____

hand

Fill in the Sentence

Fill in the blanks to make the word **hand**.

My ____ ____ ____ ____ was on the door.

His ____ ____ ____ ____ is bigger than mine.

Her ____ ____ ____ ____ is soft.

Circle the Word

Circle the flowers that have the word **hand**.

Circle the Word in the Sentence

Circle the word **hand** in the sentences.

Please hold my hand.   What is in her hand?

have

Sight Word Practice: Have

Write the word: **have**

_____   _____

_____   _____

_____   _____

Fill in the Sentence

Fill in the blanks to make the word **have**.

I _____ _____ _____ _____

two sisters.

The boys _____ _____ _____ _____

gone home.

We _____ _____ _____ _____

seen the moon in the sky.

Circle the Word

Circle the flowers that have the word **have**.

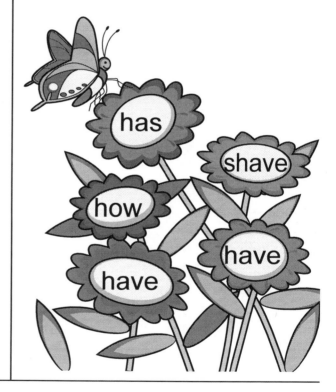

Circle the Word in the Sentence

Circle the word **have** in the sentences.

Do you have a hat? They have sung that song before.

Sight Word Practice: He

Write the Word: he

_____   _____

- - - - - - - - - - - - - - - - -

_____   _____

Fill in the Sentence

Fill in the blanks to make the word **he**.

_____ _____ likes my cat.

Where is _____ _____ going?

We will go when _____ _____ gets here.

Circle the Word

Circle the flowers that have the word **he**.

Circle the Word in the Sentence

Circle the word **he** in the sentences.

He is my friend.   Can he come to my house?

Sight Word Practice: Head

Write the Word: **head**

_____ _____

_____ _____

_____ _____

Fill in the Sentence

Fill in the blanks to make the word **head**.

He put his ____ ____ ____ ____

down.

My ____ ____ ____ ____ is cold.

I patted the dog on its

____ ____ ____ ____ .

Circle the Word

Circle the flowers that have the word **head**.

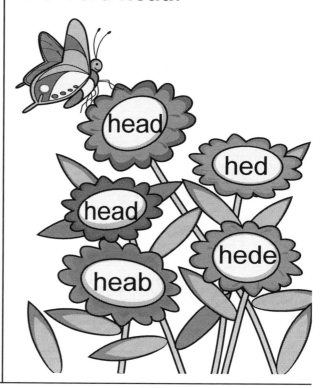

Circle the Word in the Sentence

Circle the word **head** in the sentences.

She hurt her head.   The hat was on his head.

help

Sight Word Practice: Help

Write the Word: **help**

_____ _____
- - - - - - - - - - - - - - -
_____ _____

Fill in the Sentence

Fill in the blanks to make the word **help**.

She will ____ ____ ____ ____ us today.

He called for ____ ____ ____ ____ when he fell.

Please ____ ____ ____ ____ me with the chores.

Circle the Word

Circle the flowers that have the word **help**.

Circle the Word in the Sentence

Circle the word **help** in the sentences.

The man can not help her.

Do you need some help with that?

Name: _____

Sight Word Practice: Here

Write the Word: **here**

here

_____ _____

_ _ _ _ _ _ _ _ _ _ _ _ _

_____ _____

Fill in the Sentence

Fill in the blanks to make the word **here**.

She came ____ ____ ____ ____ to say hello.

____ ____ ____ ____ is my book.

Put the pencils

____ ____ ____ ____ .

Circle the Word

Circle the flowers that have the word **here**.

Circle the Word in the Sentence

Circle the word **here** in the sentences.

The store is near here.

How long has she been here?

55

Name: _____

Sight Word Practice: I

Write the Word: I

_____   _____

------------------   ------------------

_____   _____

Fill in the Sentence

Fill in the blanks to make the word I.

_____ walked home.

_____ saw a bird.

That house is where _____ live.

Circle the Word

Circle the flowers that have the word I.

Circle the Word in the Sentence

Circle the word **I** in the sentences.

She liked what I made.   I went to the store.

Name: _____

Sight Word Practice: In

Write the Word: **in**

_____   _____
- - - - - - - - - - -   - - - - - - - - - - -
_____   _____

Fill in the Sentence

Fill in the blanks to make the word **in**.

They walked _____ _____
the house.

The bell rings _____ _____
an hour.

He will run _____ _____
the race.

Circle the Word

Circle the flowers that have the word **in**.

Circle the Word in the Sentence

Circle the word **in** in the sentences.

The girl put the cup in the box.

There is a frog in my bed!

Name: _____

Sight Word Practice: Into

Write the Word: **into**

into

- - - - - - - - - - - - - - - - -

- - - - - - - - - - - - - - - - -

- - - - - - - - - - - - - - - - -

Fill in the Sentence

Fill in the blanks to make the word **into**.

The man walked

_____ _____ _____ _____ the room.

They put the boat

_____ _____ _____ _____ the water.

He ran his bike

_____ _____ _____ _____ a tree.

Circle the Word

Circle the flowers that have the word **into**.

Circle the Word in the Sentence

Circle the word **into** in the sentences.

The moth turned into a butterfly.

We went into the house.

is

Name: _____

Sight Word Practice: Is

Write the Word: **is**

_____ _____

- - - - - - - - - - - - - - - - - - - - - -

_____ _____

Fill in the Sentence

Fill in the blanks to make the word **is**.

He _____ _____ late for dinner.

The cat _____ _____ funny.

The horse _____ _____

jumping the fence.

Circle the Word

Circle the flowers that have the word **is**.

Circle the Word in the Sentence

Circle the word **is** in the sentences.

She is singing a song.   The hat is on my head.

Name: _____

Sight Word Practice: It

Write the Word: **it**

_____   _____

- -

_____   _____

Fill in the Sentence

Fill in the blanks to make the word **it**.

I got _____ _____ at the store.

She put _____ _____ on the table.

_____ _____ was nice to see you.

Circle the Word

Circle the flowers that have the word **it**.

Circle the Word in the Sentence

Circle the word **it** in the sentences.

It is a pretty day.   We threw it away.

Name: _____

Sight Word Practice: Jump

Write the Word: **jump**

_____

– – – – – – – – – –

_____

– – – – – – – – – –

_____

Fill in the Sentence

Fill in the blanks to make the word **jump**.

She can ____ ____ ____ ____ very high.

We saw the frog

____ ____ ____ ____ over the rock.

I like to ____ ____ ____ ____ and run.

Circle the Word

Circle the flowers that have the word **jump**.

Circle the Word in the Sentence

Circle the word **jump** in the sentences.

Don't jump on the bed!   Can you jump over that?

Sight Word Practice: Like

Write the Word: **like**

like _ _ _ _ _ _ _ _ _ _ _ _

Fill in the Sentence

Fill in the blanks to make the word **like**.

I ____ ____ ____ ____ bananas.

She had a hat

____ ____ ____ ____ his.

The dog looked

____ ____ ____ ____ a wolf.

Circle the Word

Circle the flowers that have the word **like**.

Circle the Word in the Sentence

Circle the word **like** in the sentences.

Can you walk like a duck?

They will like the show.

Name: _____

Sight Word Practice: Little

Write the Word: **little**

_____

- - - - - - - - - - - - - - - - -

_____

- - - - - - - - - - - - - - - - -

Fill in the Sentence

Fill in the blanks to make the word **little**.

The shoes were too

____ ___ ____ ____ ____ ____ ____.

We saw

____ ____ ____ ____ ____ ____ ____

kittens on the farm.

I will have a

____ ____ ____ ____ ____ ____ ____

pie.

Circle the Word

Circle the flowers that have the word **little**.

Circle the Word in the Sentence

Circle the word **little** in the sentences.

The little dog was nice.

The ride was a little scary.

Name: _____

Sight Word Practice: Look

Write the Word: **look**

look

----------- -----------

----------- -----------

----------- -----------

Fill in the Sentence

Fill in the blanks to make the word **look**.

We will ____ ____ ____ ____ for your cat.

He did not ____ ____ ____ ____ happy.

She will ____ ____ ____ ____ pretty in that dress.

Circle the Word

Circle the flowers that have the word **look**.

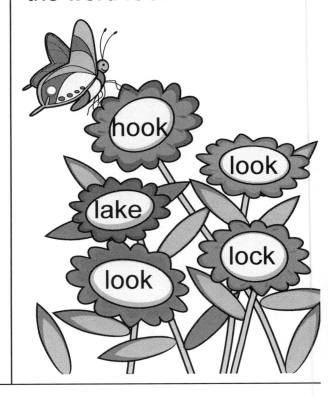

Circle the Word in the Sentence

Circle the word **look** in the sentences.

Look at the funny hat!   Did you look at the book?

Name: _____

Sight Word Practice: Make

Write the Word: **make**

make

Fill in the Sentence

Fill in the blanks to make the word **make**.

I shall ____ ____ ____ ____
a cake.

She will ____ ____ ____ ____
good grades this year.

My dog can ____ ____ ____ ____
a lot of noise.

Circle the Word

Circle the flowers that have the word **make**.

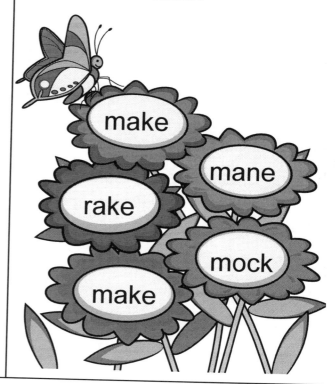

Circle the Word in the Sentence

Circle the word **make** in the sentences.

What do you make of that?

The paint may make a mess on the floor.

Name: _____

Sight Word Practice: Man

Write the Word: **man**

man

_____ _____

_____ _____

Fill in the Sentence

Fill in the blanks to make the word **man**.

The _____ _____ _____ walked down the road.

They asked the _____ _____ _____ for food.

The tall _____ _____ _____ sang a song.

Circle the Word

Circle the flowers that have the word **man**.

Circle the Word in the Sentence

Circle the word **man** in the sentences.

That man lives next door to us.   They saw a man on the bus.

Name: _____

Sight Word Practice: Me

Write the Word: **me**

me -------------------------- --------------------------

Fill in the Sentence

Fill in the blanks to make the word **me**.

She gave ____ ____ a hat.

I want you to tell ____ ____ a story.

He will not talk to ____ ____.

Circle the Word

Circle the flowers that have the word **me**.

Circle the Word in the Sentence

Circle the word **me** in the sentences.

My mother told me to come home.

Did you see me at the park?

Name: _____

Sight Word Practice: My

Write the Word: **my**

my - - - - - - - - -   - - - - - - - - -

- - - - - - - - -   - - - - - - - - -

Fill in the Sentence

Fill in the blanks to make the word **my**.

This is ____ ____ mother.

We can play at ____ ____ house.

We saw ____ ____ cat in the tree.

Circle the Word

Circle the flowers that have the word **my**.

Circle the Word in the Sentence

Circle the word **my** in the sentences.

My bike is blue.   Where is my book?

Name: _____

Sight Word Practice: No

Write the Word: **no**

_____   _____

- -

_____   _____

Fill in the Sentence

Fill in the blanks to make the word **no**.

There was ____ ____ one home.

We had ____ ____ place to play.

____ ____ boys were on the bus.

Circle the Word

Circle the flowers that have the word **no**.

Circle the Word in the Sentence

Circle the word **no** in the sentences.

We have no pets.   Did he say no?

Name: _____

Sight Word Practice: Not

Write the word: **not**

_____   _____

_____   _____

_____   _____

Fill in the Sentence

Fill in the blanks to make the word **not**.

It will _____ _____ _____

rain today.

He does _____ _____ _____

want to play.

That is _____ _____ _____

a mouse.

Circle the Word

Circle the flowers that have the word **not**.

Circle the Word in the Sentence

Circle the word **not** in the sentences.

She wanted not one but two apples.

I do not see the dog.

Sight Word Practice: Now

Write the Word: **now**

now

_____ _____

- - - - - - - - - - - - - - - - - -

_____ _____

Fill in the Sentence

Fill in the blanks to make the word **now**.

He left the room just

_____ _____ _____.

You must go home _____ _____ _____.

I _____ _____ _____ like cabbage.

Circle the Word

Circle the flowers that have the word **now**.

Circle the Word in the Sentence

Circle the word **now** in the sentences.

She now wants a new dress.

Who wants dinner now?

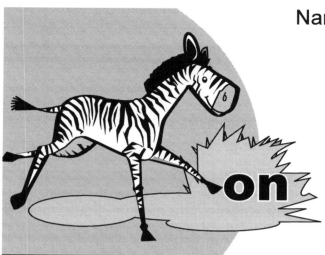

Name: _____

Sight Word Practice: On

Write the word: **on**

_____   _____

- - - - - - - - - - - - - -   - - - - - - - - - - -

_____   _____

Fill in the Sentence

Fill in the blanks to make the word **on**.

She rode _____ _____ a train.

We played _____ _____ the beach.

The boy put _____ _____ his coat.

Circle the Word

Circle the flowers that have the word **on**.

Circle the Word in the Sentence

Circle the word **on** in the sentences.

He got to the party on time.

The flowers are on the table.

Sight Word Practice: One

Write the word: **one**

one

_____ _____

_____ _____

_____ _____

Fill in the Sentence

Fill in the blanks to make the word **one**.

We read _____ _____ _____
story today.

She liked the blue _____ _____ _____ .

Do you need _____ _____ _____
or two pens?

Circle the Word

Circle the flowers that have the word **one**.

Circle the Word in the Sentence

Circle the word **one** in the sentences.

He has one cat.   I want one banana.

Name: _____

Sight Word Practice: Our

Write the Word: **our**

_____ _____

_____ _____

_____ _____

Fill in the Sentence

Fill in the blanks to make the word **our**.

We ate ____ ____ ____ lunch.

They came to ____ ____ ____ party.

She is ____ ____ ____ mother.

Circle the Word

Circle the flowers that have the word **our**.

Circle the Word in the Sentence

Circle the word **our** in the sentences.

We saw our uncle at the store.   Our dog can do a trick.

Name: _____

Sight Word Practice: Out

Write the Word: **out**

out

_ _ _ _ _ _ _ _ _ _   _ _ _ _ _ _ _ _ _ _

Fill in the Sentence

Fill in the blanks to make the word **out**.

We walked ____ ____ ____ the door.

I saw her ____ ____ ____ the window.

The dog wanted to go ____ ____ ____.

Circle the Word

Circle the flowers that have the word **out**.

Circle the Word in the Sentence

Circle the word **out** in the sentences.

He took the spoon out of the drawer.

They like to be out in the sunshine.

75

Sight Word Practice: Pig

Write the Word: **pig**

pig

Fill in the Sentence

Fill in the blanks to make the word **pig**.

The ____ ____ ____ sat in the mud.

The farmer fed the ____ ____ ____ .

That ____ ____ ____ is mine.

Circle the Word

Circle the flowers that have the word **pig**.

Circle the Word in the Sentence

Circle the word **pig** in the sentences.

The farm had a cow and a pig.   A pig has a curly tail.

Name: _____

Sight Word Practice: Play

Write the Word: **play**

_____   _____

_____   _____

_____   _____

Fill in the Sentence

Fill in the blanks to make the word **play**.

We want to ____ ____ ____ ____ in the park.

He will not ____ ____ ____ ____ today.

Let's go outside and

____ ____ ____ ____ .

Circle the Word

Circle the flowers that have the word **play**.

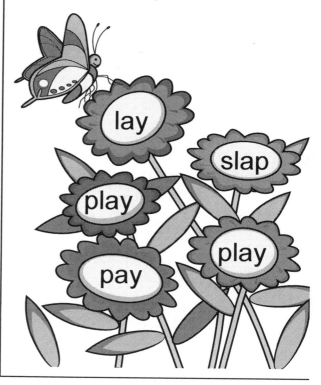

Circle the Word in the Sentence

Circle the word **play** in the sentences.

They saw a play at school.

I can play a song for you.

Name: _____

Sight Word Practice: Ran

Write the Word: **ran**

_____ _____

- -

Fill in the Sentence

Fill in the blanks to make the word **ran**.

She ____ ____ ____ to school.

The boys ____ ____ ____ a race.

The water ____ ____ ____ down the wall.

Circle the Word

Circle the flowers that have the word **ran**.

Circle the Word in the Sentence

Circle the word **ran** in the sentences.

The horse ran fast.   They ran to the door.

Name: _____

Sight Word Practice: Red

Write the Word: **red**

red

_____ _____

- - - - - - - - - - - - - - - - - -

_____ _____

Fill in the Sentence

Fill in the blanks to make the word **red**.

She wore a ____ ____ ____ dress.

The ____ ____ ____ apple looks good.

The barn was ____ ____ ____ .

Circle the Word

Circle the flowers that have the word **red**.

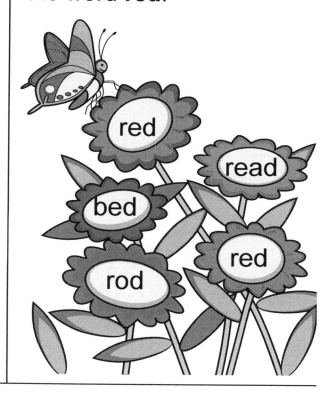

Circle the Word in the Sentence

Circle the word **red** in the sentences.

I have a red pen.

Do you want the red one or the blue one?

Name: _____

Sight Word Practice: Ride

Write the Word: **ride**

ride _____ _____

_____

Fill in the Sentence

Fill in the blanks to make the word **ride**.

They went for a

____ ____ ____ ____ on the bus.

I want to ____ ____ ____ ____ a
horse.

She will ____ ____ ____ ____ a
bike to school.

Circle the Word

Circle the flowers that have the word **ride**.

Circle the Word in the Sentence

Circle the word **ride** in the sentences.

Will you ride with us?

He likes to ride in the car.

Name: _____

Sight Word Practice: Run

Write the Word: **run**

run

_____ _____

- - - - - - - - -   - - - - - - - - -

_____ _____

Fill in the Sentence

Fill in the blanks to make the word **run**.

We must ____ ____ ____ to school.

Today they will ____ ____ ____ a race.

She can ____ ____ ____ very fast.

Circle the Word

Circle the flowers that have the word **run**.

Circle the Word in the Sentence

Circle the word **run** in the sentences.

His dog has run away.

You should not run in the house.

Sight Word Practice: Said

Write the word: **said**

_____   _____

- - - - - - - - -   - - - - - - - - -

_____   _____

Fill in the Sentence

Fill in the blanks to make the word **said**.

He _____ _____ _____ _____ he would

not be late.

I forgot what you

_____ _____ _____ _____.

They _____ _____ _____ _____

they will play at the park.

Circle the Word

Circle the flowers that have the word **said**.

Circle the Word in the Sentence

Circle the word **said** in the sentences.

She said you were funny.   What was it you said to him?

Name: _____

Sight Word Practice: See

Write the Word: **see**

see

_____   _____

_____   _____

Fill in the Sentence

Fill in the blanks to make the word **see**.

She can ____ ____ ____ the moon.

They ____ ____ ____ their aunt each week.

Let's ____ ____ ____ if he is ready.

Circle the Word

Circle the flowers that have the word **see**.

sea

see

see

seem

bee

Circle the Word in the Sentence

Circle the word **see** in the sentences.

I want to see that movie.

Can you see the light?

Name: _____

Sight Word Practice: She

Write the word: **she**

_____

_____

_____

Fill in the Sentence

Fill in the blanks to make the word **she**.

Is ____ ____ ____ the one in the red dress?

____ ____ ____ is the first one in line.

Please tell me when

____ ____ ____ gets here.

Circle the Word

Circle the flowers that have the word **she**.

Circle the Word in the Sentence

Circle the word **she** in the sentences.

She is my best friend.   Does she have a brother?

shoe

Sight Word Practice: Shoe

Write the Word: **shoe**

Fill in the Sentence

Fill in the blanks to make the word **shoe**.

I lost my _____ _____ _____ _____ .

That _____ _____ _____ _____ is red.

He took off his

_____ _____ _____ _____ .

Circle the Word

Circle the flowers that have the word **shoe**.

Circle the Word in the Sentence

Circle the word **shoe** in the sentences.

The shoe was under the bed.   She put on one shoe.

Name: _____

Sight Word Practice: Snow

Write the Word: **snow**

snow

_____   _____

_____   _____

Fill in the Sentence

Fill in the blanks to make the word **snow**.

The ____ ____ ____ ____ is white.

We played in the

____ ____ ____ ____ .

The ____ ____ ____ ____ fell outside.

Circle the Word

Circle the flowers that have the word **snow**.

now

soon

snow

snow

slow

Circle the Word in the Sentence

Circle the word **snow** in the sentences.

The snow was deep.   The dog ran in the snow.

Sight Word Practice: So

Write the Word: **so**

- -

Fill in the Sentence

Fill in the blanks to make the word **so**.

We were late, _____ _____ we had to hurry.

They were hungry, _____ _____ they ate very fast.

I was _____ _____ glad to see my grandmother.

Circle the Word

Circle the flowers that have the word **so**.

Circle the Word in the Sentence

Circle the word **so** in the sentences.

He was funny, and so was she.

She was so sorry she missed the party.

Name: _____

Sight Word Practice: Song

Write the Word: **song**

_____ _____

- -

_____ _____

Fill in the Sentence

Fill in the blanks to make the word **song**.

I like that ____ ____ ____ ____ .

The ____ ____ ____ ____ was very loud.

She does not know this

____ ____ ____ ____ .

Circle the Word

Circle the flowers that have the word **song**.

Circle the Word in the Sentence

Circle the word **song** in the sentences.

He sang a song.   What is the name of that song?

Name: _____

Sight Word Practice: Sun

Write the Word: sun

sun

_____ _____

_____ _____

Fill in the Sentence

Fill in the blanks to make the word **sun**.

He saw the ____ ____ ____ come up .

The ____ ____ ____ is in the sky.

The ____ ____ ____ helps the plants grow.

Circle the Word

Circle the flowers that have the word **sun**.

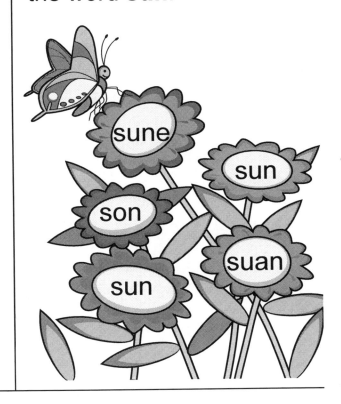

Circle the Word in the Sentence

Circle the word **sun** in the sentences.

The sun was bright today.   We watched the sun go down.

Name: _____

Sight Word Practice: that

Write the Word: **that**

_____   _____

- - - - - - - - - - - -   - - - - - - - - - - - -

_____   _____

Fill in the Sentence

Fill in the blanks to make the word **that**.

Look at ____ ____ ____ ____ cow.

I love ____ ____ ____ ____ song.

We should walk

____ ____ ____ ____ way.

Circle the Word

Circle the flowers that have the word **that**.

Circle the Word in the Sentence

Circle the word **that** in the sentences.

Here is the pie that you like.   That boy is my brother.

Name: _____

Sight Word Practice: The

Write the Word: **the**

_____   _____

- - - - - - - - -   - - - - - - - - -

_____   _____

Fill in the Sentence

Fill in the blanks to make the word **the**.

She ate _____ _____ _____ apple.

I like _____ _____ _____ book.

He walked in _____ _____ _____ store.

Circle the Word

Circle the flowers that have the word **the**.

Circle the Word in the Sentence

Circle the word **the** in the sentences.

The boy ran to the park.   We saw the cat.

Name: _____

Sight Word Practice: There

Write the word: **there**

_____ _____

_____ _____

there

Fill in the Sentence

Fill in the blanks to make the word **there**.

____ ____ ____ ____ ____ are no

apples left.

Can you run over

____ ____ ____ ____ ____?

He went ____ ____ ____ ____ ____

with his brother.

Circle the Word

Circle the flowers that have the word **there**.

Circle the Word in the Sentence

Circle the word **there** in the sentences.

There was a fly in their soup.

She will not go there again.

Name: _____

Sight Word Practice: They

Write the word: **they**

they

---- ----

---- ----

---- ----

Fill in the Sentence

Fill in the blanks to make the word **they**.

We can play until ____ ____ ____ get here.

____ ____ ____ ____ are singing to me.

Do ____ ____ ____ know where to go?

Circle the Word

Circle the flowers that have the word **they**.

Circle the Word in the Sentence

Circle the word **they** in the sentences.

Are they here yet?   They ate dinner with us.

Name: _____

Sight Word Practice: This

Write the word: **this**

_____ _____

- - - - - - - - - - - - - - - -

_____ _____

Fill in the Sentence

Fill in the blanks to make the word **this**.

She wants _____ _____ _____ _____ toy.

_____ _____ _____ _____ is my school.

I will read _____ _____ _____ _____ book.

Circle the Word

Circle the flowers that have the word **this**.

Circle the Word in the Sentence

Circle the word **this** in the sentences.

Is this your coat?   This cup is hers.

Name: _____

Sight Word Practice: Three

Write the Word: **three**

_____

_____

_____

_____

Fill in the Sentence

Fill in the blanks to make the word **three**.

He saw

____ ____ ____ ____ ____ birds.

The ____ ____ ____ ____ ____

books are on the floor.

We went to

____ ____ ____ ____ ____ stores.

Circle the Word

Circle the flowers that have the word **three**.

here

tree

three

three

there

Circle the Word in the Sentence

Circle the word **three** in the sentences.

She has three pens.   Can you count to three?

Name: _____

Sight Word Practice: To

Write the Word: **to**

_____   _____

- -

_____   _____

Fill in the Sentence

Fill in the blanks to make the word **to**.

She went _____ _____ the store.

I gave the pie _____ _____ her.

They want _____ _____ go with us.

Circle the Word

Circle the flowers that have the word **to**.

Circle the Word in the Sentence

Circle the word **to** in the sentences.

We will go to the park.   He likes to run fast.

Name: _____

Sight Word Practice: Top

Write the Word: **top**

top

_____   _____

_____   _____

_____   _____

Fill in the Sentence

Fill in the blanks to make the word **top**.

The _____ _____ _____ book is mine.

We went to the _____ _____ _____ of the hill.

The bird flew to the _____ _____ _____ of the tree.

Circle the Word

Circle the flowers that have the word **top**.

Circle the Word in the Sentence

Circle the word **top** in the sentences.

The cat is on top of the roof.

The pan is on the top shelf.

Sight Word Practice: Toy

Write the Word: **toy**

_____ _____

- -

_____ _____

Fill in the Sentence

Fill in the blanks to make the word **toy**.

He gave her a ____ ____ ____ .

The ____ ____ ____ was in a box.

My ____ ____ ____ car is lost.

Circle the Word

Circle the flowers that have the word **toy**.

Circle the Word in the Sentence

Circle the word **toy** in the sentences.

The boy had a new toy.   That toy is green.

Name: _____

Sight Word Practice: Tree

Write the Word: **tree**

_____ _____

___ ___ ___ ___ ___ ___ ___ ___

_____ _____

Fill in the Sentence

Fill in the blanks to make the word **tree**.

The big ____ ____ ____ ____

fell over.

We sat under the

____ ____ ____ ____ .

That ____ ____ ____ ____ is tall.

Circle the Word

Circle the flowers that have the word **tree**.

Circle the Word in the Sentence

Circle the word **tree** in the sentences.

The cat ran up the tree.   The tree grew very slowly.

Name: _____

Sight Word Practice: Two

Write the Word: **two**

two

_____   _____

- - - - - - - - -   - - - - - - - - -

_____   _____

Fill in the Sentence

Fill in the blanks to make the word **two**.

I have ____ ____ ____ cats.

The ____ ____ ____ boys ran here.

She ate ____ ____ ____ apples.

Circle the Word

Circle the flowers that have the word **two**.

Circle the Word in the Sentence

Circle the word **two** in the sentences.

We called two times.   The two dogs barked.

Sight Word Practice: Up

Write the word: **up**

up

_____   _____

- - - - - - - - - - -   - - - - - - - - - - -

_____   _____

Fill in the Sentence

Fill in the blanks to make the word **up**.

We went _____ _____ the street to the store.

The mouse ran _____ _____ the clock.

The dog chased the cat _____ _____ a tree.

Circle the Word

Circle the flowers that have the word **up**.

Circle the Word in the Sentence

Circle the word **up** in the sentences.

We ran up the stairs.   She looked up at the moon.

want

Name: _____

Sight Word Practice: Want

Write the Word: **want**

_____   _____

- - - - - - - - - -   - - - - - - - - - -

_____   _____

Fill in the Sentence

Fill in the blanks to make the word **want**.

They ____ ____ ____ ____ to stay here.

I ____ ____ ____ ____ to sing a song.

We ____ ____ ____ ____ to go home.

Circle the Word

Circle the flowers that have the word **want**.

Circle the Word in the Sentence

Circle the word **want** in the sentences.

She may want to go with us.   Do you want an apple?

Name: _____

Sight Word Practice: Was

Write the word: **was**

_____   _____

- - - - - - - - - - -   - - - - - - - - - - -

_____   _____

Fill in the Sentence

Fill in the blanks to make the word **was**.

Tom ____ ____ ____ on the bus.

The bird ____ ____ ____ flying across the sky.

I ____ ____ ____ late to school.

Circle the Word

Circle the flowers that have the word **was**.

Circle the Word in the Sentence

Circle the word **was** in the sentences.

She was running down the street. Was he here today?

Name: _____

Sight Word Practice: We

Write the word: we

_____   _____

_____   _____

_____   _____

Fill in the Sentence

Fill in the blanks to make the word **we**.

Tell us when _____ _____
can come in.

_____ _____ are good
students.

Do _____ _____ have
work to do?

Circle the Word

Circle the flowers that have the word **we**.

Circle the Word in the Sentence

Circle the word **we** in the sentences.

We looked at a new car.   Where are we going?

Name: _____

Sight Word Practice: Went

Write the Word: **went**

_____

_____

_____

_____

Fill in the Sentence

Fill in the blanks to make the word **went**.

He ____ ____ ____ ____ into the house.

We ____ ____ ____ ____ outside to play.

The rain began after they
____ ____ ____ ____ home.

Circle the Word

Circle the flowers that have the word **went**.

Circle the Word in the Sentence

Circle the word **went** in the sentences.

The dog went to the barn.

She went to school with me.

Name: _____

Sight Word Practice: What

Write the word: **what**

what ————————————   ————————————

Fill in the Sentence

Fill in the blanks to make the word **what**.

She liked ____ ____ ____ ____
you gave her.

____ ____ ____ ____ time is it?

Tom told me ____ ____ ____ ____
he saw.

Circle the Word

Circle the flowers that have the word **what**.

Circle the Word in the Sentence

Circle the word **what** in the sentences.

He knows what to do.   What is your name?

Sight Word Practice: Where

Write the Word: **where**

where

<hr/>

Fill in the Sentence

Fill in the blanks to make the word **where**.

I know ____ ____ ____ ____
we will go.

She knew

____ ____ ____ ____ ____ she
was.

____ ____ ____ ____ are
you?

Circle the Word

Circle the flowers that have the word **where**.

Circle the Word in the Sentence

Circle the word **where** in the sentences.

He didn't know where his shoes were.

Where did you sit?

Name: _____

Sight Word Practice: White

Write the Word: **white**

_____
_____
_____
_____

Fill in the Sentence

Fill in the blanks to make the word **white**.

The clouds in the sky were

____ ____ ____ ____ ____.

The ____ ____ ____ ____ ____
bird flew to the tree.

____ ____ ____ ____
snowflakes fell on her nose.

Circle the Word

Circle the flowers that have the word **white**.

Circle the Word in the Sentence

Circle the word **white** in the sentences.

My kitten is brown and white.

He drew a blue line on the white paper.

Name: _____

Sight Word Practice: Will

Write the word: **will**

_____   _____

_____   _____

_____   _____

Fill in the Sentence

Fill in the blanks to make the word **will**.

We ____ ____ ____ ____ be there later.

When ____ ____ ____ ____ you wear your hat?

I ____ ____ ____ ____ eat lunch soon.

Circle the Word

Circle the flowers that have the word **will**.

Circle the Word in the Sentence

Circle the word **will** in the sentences.

Will you call me today?   He will sing at the show.

Name: _____

Sight Word Practice: With

Write the word: **with**

_____   _____

_____   _____

_____

Fill in the Sentence

Fill in the blanks to make the word **with**.

She danced ____ ____ ____ ____ him.

They cried ____ ____ ____ ____ joy.

The boy ____ ____ ____ ____ the cap is my friend.

Circle the Word

Circle the flowers that have the word **with**.

Circle the Word in the Sentence

Circle the word **with** in the sentences.

I went with her to the store.   He is angry with me.

Name: _____

Sight Word Practice: Yellow

Write the Word: **yellow**

_____

_____

_____

_____

yellow

Fill in the Sentence

Fill in the blanks to make the word **yellow**.

The sun is

___ ___ ___ ___ ___ .

He wore

___ ___ ___ ___ ___ ___

socks.

The

___ ___ ___ ___ ___ ___

duck walked away.

Circle the Word

Circle the flowers that have the word **yellow**.

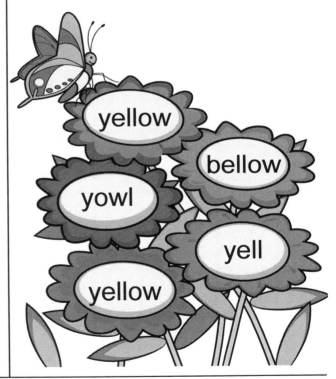

yellow
bellow
yowl
yell
yellow

Circle the Word in the Sentence

Circle the word **yellow** in the sentences.

She ate a yellow banana.

I have a yellow pencil.

Name: _____

Sight Word Practice: Yes

Write the Word: **yes**

yes - - - - - - - - - - - - - - - - - - - - - - - - - -

Fill in the Sentence

Fill in the blanks to make the word **yes**.

He will tell us ____ ____ ____ or no.

____ ____ ____, I can do that!

The answer is ____ ____ ____.

Circle the Word

Circle the flowers that have the word **yes**.

Circle the Word in the Sentence

Circle the word **yes** in the sentences.

Yes, it is hot today.

Do you think she will say yes?

Name: _____

Sight Word Practice: You

Write the Word: **you**

_____   _____

- - - - - - - - - - - - - - - - - -

_____   _____

Fill in the Sentence

Fill in the blanks to make the word **you**.

Do _____ _____ _____

want some water?

I want _____ _____ _____ to

come with me.

We will do what

_____ _____ _____ want.

Circle the Word

Circle the flowers that have the word **you**.

Circle the Word in the Sentence

Circle the word **you** in the sentences.

Are you going to the store?   You look nice today.

Multiple Word Activities

Name: _____

Animal Fun: Circle the Word "For"

Circle all the animals that have the word **for** on them.
When you are finished, you may color the picture.

Name: _____

Animal Fun: Circle the Word "Get"

Circle all the animals that have the word **get** on them.
When you are finished, you may color the picture.

Name: _____

Animal Fun: Circle the Word "Not"

Circle all the animals that have the word **not** on them.
When you are finished, you may color the picture.

Animal Fun: Circle the Word "Run"

Circle all the animals that have the word **run** on them.
When you are finished, you may color the picture.

Animal Fun: Circle the Word "You"

Circle all the animals that have the word **you** on them.
When you are finished, you may color the picture.

Color the Sight Word: And

Color yellow all the spaces with the word **and**. You may color the other word spaces any color you like.

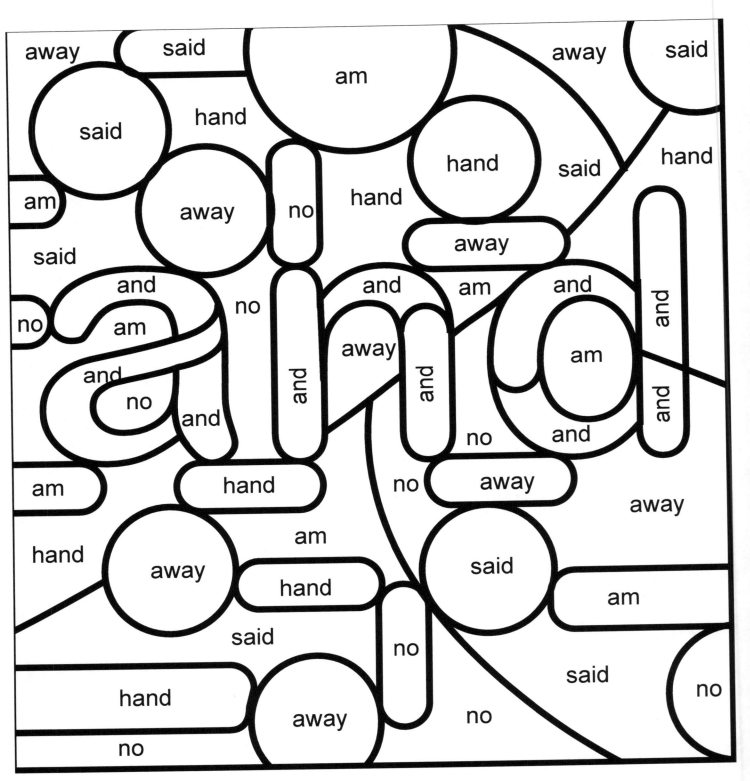

Color the Sight Word: Are

Color yellow all the spaces with the word **are**. You may color the other word spaces any color you like.

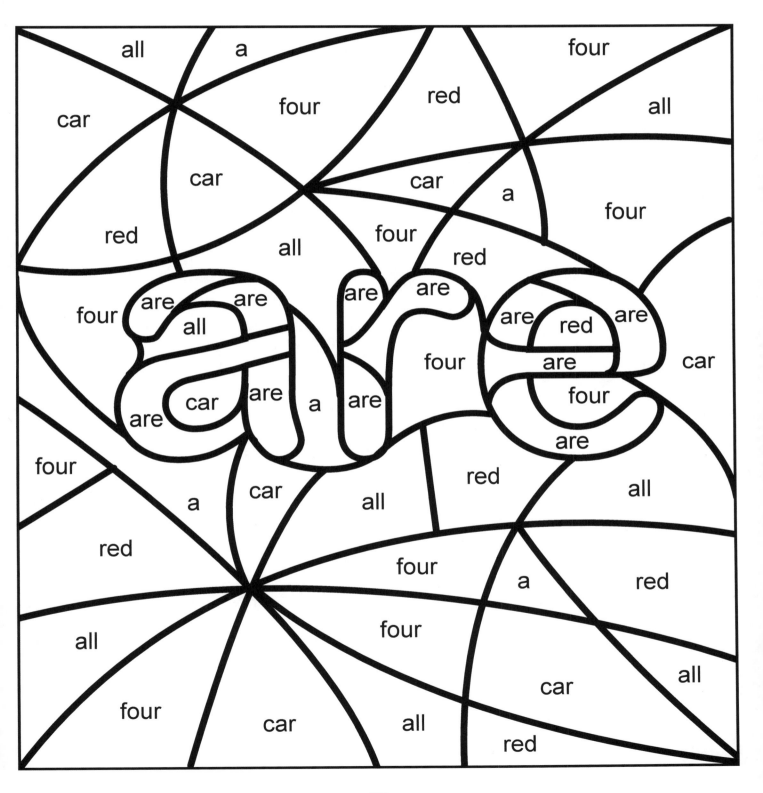

Color the Sight Word: Is

Color yellow all the spaces with the word **is**. You may color the other word spaces any color you like.

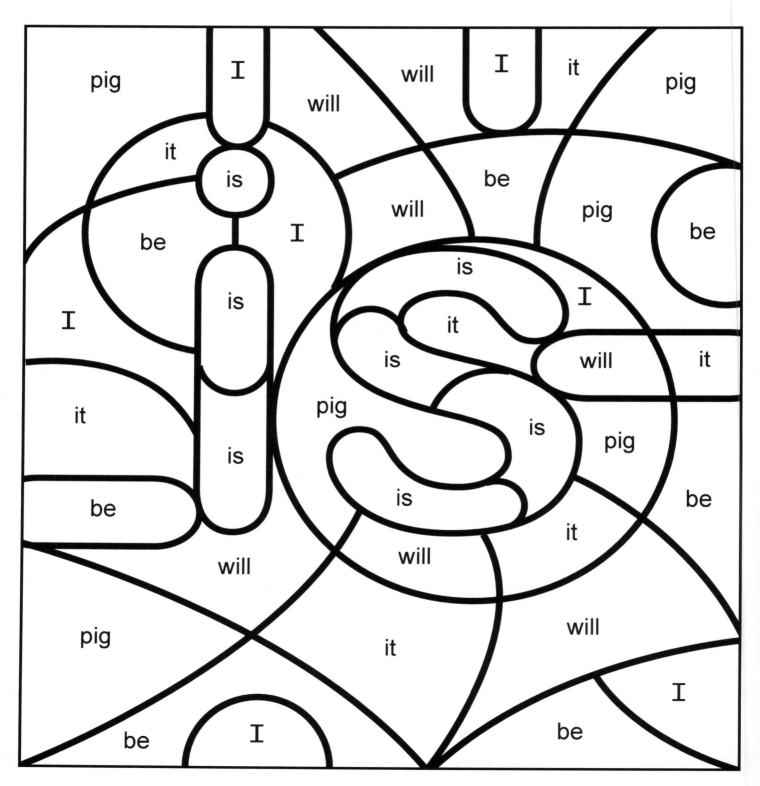

Name: _____

Color the Sight Word: The

Color yellow all the spaces with the word **the**. You may color the other word spaces any color you like.

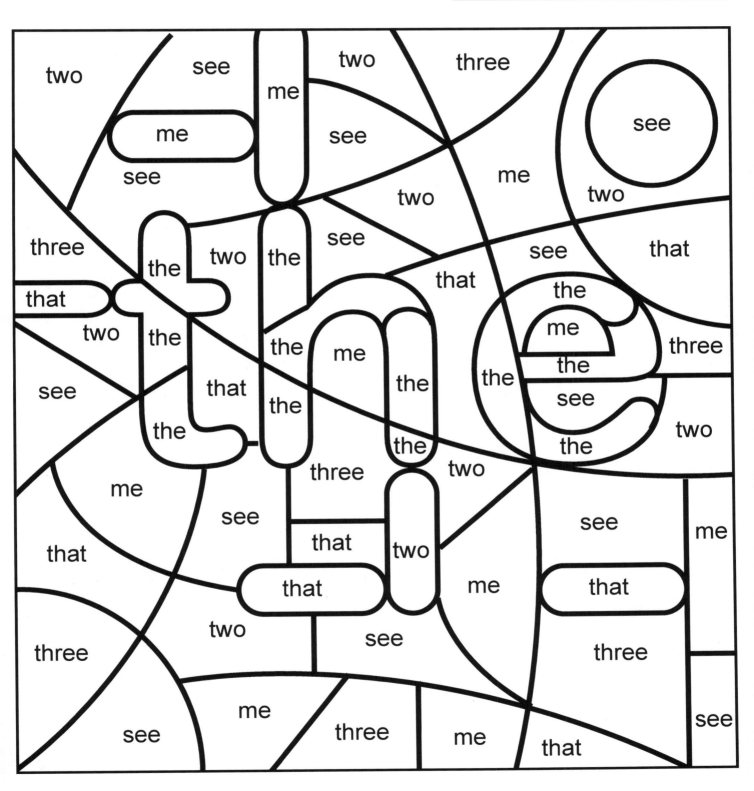

Name: _____

Color the Sight Word: Was

Color yellow all the spaces with the word **was**. You may
color the other word spaces any color you like.

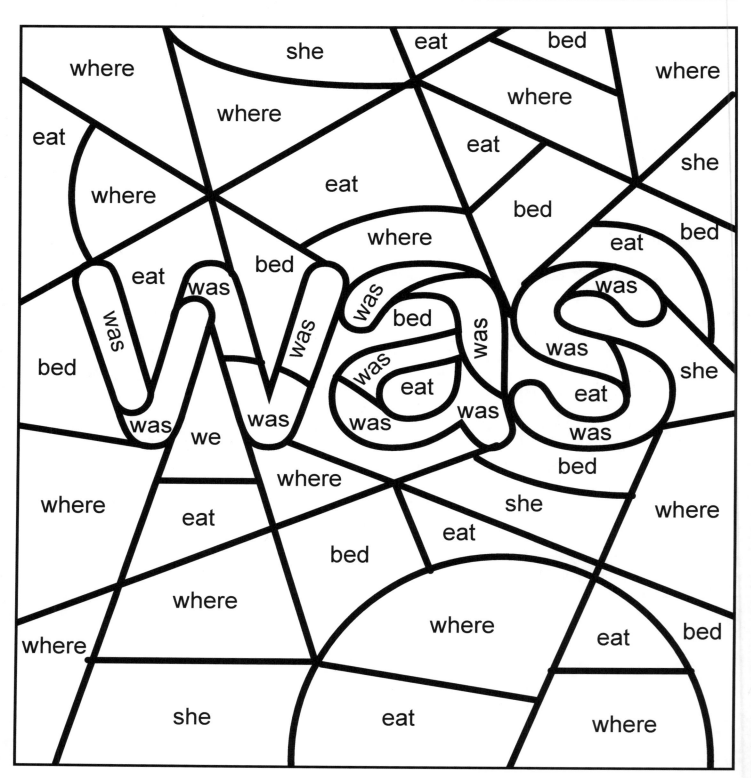

Name: _____

Sight Word Color by Number: The Cheetah

Each word in the picture stands for a color. Use the color key to find the right color to color the word spaces.

Sight word color key: 1. went = orange 2. ball = yellow 3. girl = green 4. help = blue 5. do = red 6. top = tan

Name: _____

Sight Word Color by Number: The Crocodile

Each word in the picture stands for a color. Use the color key to find the right color to color the word spaces.

Sight word color key: 1. they = light green   2. dog = tan   3. head = light blue
4. out = dark green   5. did = dark blue   6. on = yellow

Name: _____

Sight Word Color by Number: The Elephant

Each word in the picture stands for a color. Use the color key to find the right color to color the word spaces.

Sight word color key: 1. have = gray 2. cake = tan 3. boy = light blue 4. find = light green 5. yes = blue 6. up = green

Sight Word Color by Number: The Gorilla

Each word in the picture stands for a color. Use the color key to find the right color to color the word spaces.

Sight word color key: 1. here = blue   2. baby = orange   3. fire = purple
4. good = lt green   5. our = dark green   6. so = gray

Sight Word Color by Number: The Lion

Each word in the picture stands for a color. Use the color key to find the right color to color the word spaces.

Sight word color key:

1. my = orange   2. cat = light green   3. he = brown
4. play = dark green   5. go = yellow   6. duck = blue

Name: _____

Spot the Sight Words 1

There are two words above each sentence. Circle
those words in the sentence.

1. funny   yellow

He has a funny yellow hat.

2. make   to

I want to make two cakes.

3. at   funny

We laughed at the funny clown.

4. yellow   to

They walked to the yellow house.

5. at   make

She will make an A at school.

Spot the Sight Words 2

There are two words above each sentence. Circle those words in the sentence.

1. blue   big

She has a big blue car.

2. in   snow

The boy played in the snow.

3. want   blue

I want the blue pencil.

4. in   big

The big dog is in the house.

5. want   snow

They want it to snow today.

Spot the Sight Words 3

There are two words above each sentence. Circle those words in the sentence.

1. brown   came

The brown cow came into the barn.

2. song   like

They like that song.

3. what   brown

What is the name of the brown horse?

4. came   song

He came to sing us a song.

5. what   like

I like what you said.

Spot the Sight Words 4

There are two words above each sentence. Circle those words in the sentence.

1. black   can

The black dog can run fast.

2. little   there

There is a little bird.

3. black   with

The girl played with the black cat.

4. can   little

The little boy can help us.

5. there   with

I went there with my mother.

Spot the Sight Words 5

There are two words above each sentence. Circle
those words in the sentence.

1. down   white

The white duck walked down the road.

2. look   this

She can look at this book soon.

3. white   tree

The tree was white with snow.

4. this   down

This car went down the hill.

5. tree   look

I will look for the cat in the tree.

Made in the USA
San Bernardino, CA
10 March 2017